ROB HERWIG

128 HOUSEPLANTS YOU CAN GROW

With color photographs of each,
plus 12 black-and-white photographs

Collier Books, New York, New York

Translated by Irene Cumming Kleeberg
All photographs by Rob Herwig

The Macmillan Company
866 Third Avenue, New York, N.Y. 10022
Collier - Macmillan Canada Ltd., Toronto, Ontario

Originally published by L. J. Veen's Uitgeversmaatschappij N.V., Wageningen, under the title *Het kleine kamerplantenboek*

Library of Congress Catalog Card Number: 72-80070

First Collier Books Edition 1972
Second Printing

Printed in the Netherlands

Foreword

If you buy houseplants only to see them wither and die, and then have to throw them away after a few weeks, you don't need this book. I intend to give you tips for the care and maintenance of your plants so that you can prolong their life and keep them glowing with good health. This is not always easy, but it is very satisfying to a plant lover, and you will see what I mean when your first azalea opens its little buds.

There are many suitable plants for your home — the only question is which ones to choose, and once you do choose, how to keep them growing and beautiful. Plants must be comfortable and must have the right environment in order to flourish. If a plant is placed only a yard or so away from the window, it may not thrive the way it would on the windowsill. You should be aware of each plant's light requirements, and you should also know how much water, humidity, and heat, as well as what type of soil, your plants will need.

This book has special symbols, which enable you to see at a glance if your home is right for a specific plant. If you will study the key to the symbols on the inside front cover and the first few pages, you will learn more about these important growth conditions than you probably would from a long lecture on the subject, or from a thick, scholarly volume.

A final tip: don't forget that success with houseplants means using the right soil mixture, repotting the plant when necessary, and giving it the correct amounts of fertilizer and water. And now, happy growing!

Rob Herwig

Light

Sufficient light is very important to the good health of your houseplants. Plants are often placed too far from the light – in the middle of the room – and most plants won't be very happy with that treatment. There is less light even one yard from the window than there is on the windowsill, as you can measure for yourself with a light meter (*photo, upper left*). Some plants can be given too much light; full sun can be damaging. It may be best to have venetian blinds on your windows so that you can adjust the amount of light yourself (*photo, upper right*).

In this book, each plant is given one or more light symbols. You can immediately tell where best to place your plants. The meanings are as follows:

Likes full sun if possible. Have no curtains or blinds between the window and the plant.

Likes moderate daylight. If you place this plant in front of a window with southern exposure, have a curtain or blind between the window and the plant between 10 and 4 on sunny days. Windows facing east and west do not need this screening.

Likes a rather dark location. This can vary from a tree-shaded window to a spot a few yards from a light window.

Temperature

Tropical plants require a high temperature throughout the year. Succulents, cacti, and many other plants like warmth in summer but moderate coolness in winter. In modern dwellings this can often be a problem, but you should try to find a solution. Plants flourish much better at the proper (or natural) temperature. The photos opposite show a box of cacti in their summer location (a cool garage) and in their winter location (the house). The desired summer temperature is shown in this book by the following symbols:

Warm. Minimum 60–65° F.; with sufficient light, the temperature may reach 85° F. During a rest period the temperature can be somewhat lower.

Medium. Minimum 50–55° F.; maximum 65–70° F., if care is given to provide adequate ventilation.

Cold. Minimum 40–45° F. at night; maximum 55–60° F. The plants need fresh air and in the summer are at their best outdoors.

Water

It's impossible to say exactly how much water a plant needs. That usually depends on the temperature of the room, the kind of pot (earthenware or plastic), and the size of the plant. The best way to determine how much moisture is in the earth is to touch it with your finger (*photo*, *left*). Usually, you should avoid letting the pot stand in a saucer filled with water (*photo*, *right*) because then the soil will become too wet. The plant that is the best-known exception to this is the Cyperus.

Because tap water can be very hard and sometimes contains dangerous salts, rain water is often used. If the rain water is polluted, use a tap water purified by running it through a fine filter. The ordinary household water softeners, based on a change in ions, offer no improvement.

The symbols mean:

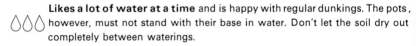 **Likes a lot of water at a time** and is happy with regular dunkings. The pots, however, must not stand with their base in water. Don't let the soil dry out completely between waterings.

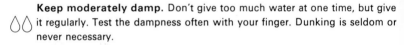 **Keep moderately damp.** Don't give too much water at one time, but give it regularly. Test the dampness often with your finger. Dunking is seldom or never necessary.

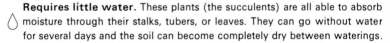 **Requires little water.** These plants (the succulents) are all able to absorb moisture through their stalks, tubers, or leaves. They can go without water for several days and the soil can become completely dry between waterings.

Humidity

In most rooms the air is too dry for houseplants. Many beautiful plants which look lovely at the nursery or florist shop can be kept alive only a short time at home. Spraying with water is often a help (*photo*, *left*), as are placing a pan of water below the plant (*photo*, *right*), a wide windowsill (less direct dry air), or, especially, an enclosed flower window.

We use the following symbols:

Needs a high humidity, which is difficult to provide in a heated room in the winter. Really a greenhouse plant, but can be successfully kept in the home during the summer.

Needs moderate humidity. The plant will do well in most rooms, even when there is central heating, provided it doesn't stand in too dry a draft and is sprayed often.

Accepts dry air very well. Suitable for very dry, unfavorable locations.

Soil

Many plants grow very well in the readily available, prepackaged nursery soil; but for those plants that strongly favor an acid or alkaline soil, you will do better to mix it yourself. In the photo on the left are shown the ingredients for a very acid growing medium: prepackaged soil and peat moss. Use about half of each. On the right you see how to mix a more alkaline, lighter mixture. The prepackaged soil is combined with 30 percent sand and, for each pound of the mixture, about $\frac{1}{2}$ ounce of lime is added. Both mixtures should be thoroughly stirred.

Experienced gardeners also achieve success by adding loam, leaf meal, compost, and the like to their plant mixtures.

Orchids, and some bromeliads, which in a natural state grow on trees, desire or even require a very special mixture. Ask your nursery for the right mixture or look it up in a book devoted to those plants.

Repotting

C   **Requires acid soil.** The use of a packaged houseplant soil, with a pH (ratio of acid to alkaline) of 4 to 5, is fine.

K   **Requires an alkaline soil.** Mix ordinary houseplant soil with some extra lime and sand, or use a special mixture containing clay or loam.

L   **Requires a very light, acid soil.** This is used for orchids, bromeliads, and similar plants. See the explanation in the text.

Not only are the minerals in the soil of a potted plant quickly exhausted, but the soil itself often gets polluted with harmful salts from tap water, an oversupply of certain fertilizers, and other chemicals. Therefore, most plants should be repotted every year, preferably in the spring. Only very old or very slow-growing plants can continue to survive in the same soil. For the plants that need a damp soil (see the symbols) I advise a plastic pot. In other cases, clay pots are more practical, because too much water often accumulates in plastic pots. Any pot you use must have a hole in the bottom so that any excess water can run out.

To repot a plant, slip it out of the old flowerpot by holding it upside down (*photo, left*). If it doesn't come out, break the pot. Now take a somewhat larger pot, and over the hole at the bottom place a piece of broken pot. Working carefully so as to do as little damage as possible to the roots, lightly knead the old soil clump so that most of the old earth falls off. Then put a little of the new soil in the bottom of the pot, set the plant on top, and pack more new soil around it. When the plant is firmly in place, sprinkle a thin layer of new earth on top of the soil already in the pot. There should be $\frac{1}{2}$-$\frac{3}{4}$ inch between the soil and the top of the pot for easy watering. After repotting, it's a good idea to prune a little of the top part of the plant to minimize surface evaporation. Keep the repotted plant out of the sun for a few weeks.

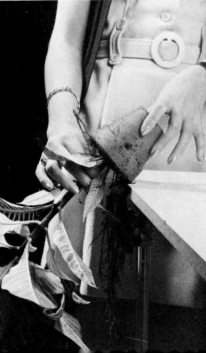

Abutilon (Flowering Maple) ►

The most beautiful is probably the pictured A. striatum Thomsonii. The spots on the leaves are caused by a virus which does not affect the plant's growth. In a large pot or tub this plant can easily become 6-10 feet tall. The Abutilon will bloom only if placed in full light. Fertilize well and also give a tablespoonful of lime now and then. The plant can summer outside, but during the winter it requires a temperature of at least 50° F. Because the plant grows quickly, it requires a great deal of food. Therefore fertilize it regularly during the summer and, above all, repot it when necessary. Within a rather short time the plant will do better in a fairly large tub. Propagate with cuttings; these will root in water.

Achimenes ►►

A richly blooming plant which requires special attention. In the autumn, give less water until the leaves die. Keep the rhizome (the underground stem, or rootstock) in a very dry pot during the winter at a temperature of 60-65° F. Repot in March (ordinary prepared houseplant soil can be used, but it is better to add a little peat moss to it) and start the plant growing again, pruning the taller types a little. Air that is too dry and water that is too alkaline are both bad for this plant. Propagate by division of the rhizomes or by cuttings.

Adiantum (Maidenhair Fern) ►

Beautiful ferns with almost-black leaf stalks. In a heated room regular spraying is necessary; it is also a good idea, during the winter, to place the plant in a somewhat cooler location. There are many different forms, not all equally strong. Generally used in window boxes, but not long-lasting. If, as a result of dry air, the plant becomes less attractive, you may perhaps save it by giving it less water for about a month. Cut off the old leaves. After this rest, give it more water, dunk it a few times, and fertilize it regularly so that new foliage is formed. Propagate by division.

Agave (Century Plant) ►►

A strong succulent plant which is grown outdoors in the south of Europe, where it becomes very large. The pictured A. americana is the most common. In the winter, keep at 40° F. and give almost no water. It can summer outside in a tub in a sheltered sunny place. If you take good care of the plant, it will reward you in a few decades with a 10-foot-tall flower stalk. Propagation is generally achieved with seeds, but it is also possible to take cuttings of young runners.

Aloe ▶

As far as care is concerned, Aloe has a great deal in common with the Agave (page 10). Therefore keep it warm and not too dry in the summer and cool in the winter, almost without water. Pictured is A. aborescens, a very strong type, which becomes very decorative as the long stem develops and puts out many side branches. In later life red flowers form, generally around Christmas. Propagate by taking off the young shoots which root easily at almost any season.

A. variegata is another, very well-known kind, a rather small plant with leaves in thick rosettes, placed askew, so the stem is not visible. On the top the leaf is hollowed out; on the bottom, it is keel-shaped; the top shows irregular, diagonal stripes. If you give A. variegata too much light, the leaves will become less green.

Anthurium ▶▶

The most common is A. scherzerianum with usually red, sometimes lighter tinted, flowers. The plants are very sensitive to cold and to hard water, and suffer from low humidity. In the winter, give the plant 6-8 weeks' rest at a temperature around 60° F., and somewhat less water.

A. andraeanum, with very large, heart-shaped leaves, is also used as a houseplant and seems to last better than A. scherzerianum. If the plant fails to bloom while new leaves continue to appear, try letting it sit in a cooler location (60° F.) for about 6 weeks before returning it to a warmer spot.

Aphelandra ▶

A beautiful houseplant that survives only when the air is sufficiently humid. There are various crosses. Most have attractively decorated leaves and yellow flowers, but some have dark-green foliage and orange flowers. Fertilize well and during the summer spray often with water. Unfortunately, it is rare for this plant to last well for long. If you wish to succeed with it, be sure to provide sufficient fertilizer.

Araucaria heterophylla (Norfolk Island Pine) ▶▶

Attractive evergreen plant for cool rooms where the humidity is not too low. After a time, the bottom branches are generally lost so that a long, bald stem develops which is not, however, unattractive. Minimum temperature in the winter should be 36-38° F., with as much light as possible. Water for this plant should contain no lime, so it is best to use rain water. Propagation succeeds only with cuttings from the top.

Asparagus ▶

A. plumosus (Asparagus Fern) is widely known as a cut plant and houseplant. The foliage is attractively divided so that the plant looks very fernlike. A. sprengeri (pictured) has coarser, asparaguslike foliage and succeeds best as a hanging plant in a moderately warm room. As the plant ages it develops white, scented flowers. This strong plant can grow well even far away from the window. It is necessary to repot the plant regularly and feed it weekly, because it grows rapidly. Dunking is advised.

Aspidistra ▶▶

A stemless, dark-green plant that grows with little light. The almost invisible flowers appear at soil level. If the leaves crack, it means that the plant is not receiving regular care. Otherwise it is a strong plant that gives few problems. The striped form, Variegata, needs more light or there will be a lack of green in the leaves. Propagate in the spring with parts of the root mass.

Asplenium ▶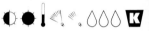

A. nidus (Bird's-nest Fern, shown in photo) forms funnel-shaped rosettes of wide leaves which show black spore groups on the underside. It is a strong plant that needs a great deal of feeding. Various other sorts, such as A. viviparum (called A. daucifolium in Europe), have feathery leaves, on which young plants develop. The young plants can be removed and grown separately.

Azalea ▶▶

Two groups are the most important: the Indian azaleas with large, generally full flowers (*photo*), and Japanese azaleas with smaller flowers. The garden variety A. mollis also is sometimes seen. While blooming, the plant must not be in too warm a location and should not receive any water containing lime. Give the plant relatively large amounts of water, especially if it is in an ordinary clay pot. It is useful to dunk it once a week. In a warm room, spray it once a week. Late-blooming varieties are the easiest to keep. Put the plant in a cooler place, but give sufficient water. You can prune the plant at the top to encourage growth at the bottom. When there is no more frost at night, place the plant in a sheltered spot in the garden, and give it a great deal of water and fertilizer through the summer. In September return it to the cool room. Regular spraying keeps the buds from falling off.

Begonia ▶

Many different kinds of begonias are suitable for houseplants. The most popular are the blooming types, which may have large or small blossoms, but these most often get mildew. Unfortunately, the beautiful leaf begonia is not always easy to raise in the home. The strongest small-flowered kind is B. semperflorens; it can also be used in the garden as a bedding plant. Larger flower forms include the Lorraine begonias, which are especially popular during the winter. There are very large flowers on plants of the Elatior type; but because they are hybrids, they are also the most sensitive.

Much stronger is a different botanical type, such as B. Cleopatra. B. x corallina, B. x erythrophylla, B. scharffiana, and various others. Sometimes these are available in florist shops, but more often you'll get them as cuttings. Proper care is very important for begonias. Keep the soil very damp (a plastic pot is best for this purpose). Once the plant becomes diseased, it usually dies. All begonias are very easy to propagate with cuttings. Cover the cutting pots with glass or plastic, so that the air remains sufficiently moist. On the other hand, if the humidity is too high, the cuttings will quickly rot; so it's important to watch the humidity in the cutting pots and to ventilate them regularly.

Begonias often grow very well for awhile, then suddenly become sick and die. Lack of light can be the cause, but it is also possible that the plant hasn't been repotted or that cuttings were not taken in time. As a rule you cannot grow the same plant longer than 2 years. Wet the leaves as little as possible and then only in the mornings.

Beloperone (Shrimp Plant) ▶

The flowers consist of deep red scales with a white crown projecting from them. This plant requires a lot of sun to grow well and doesn't thrive too well in cities due to lack of light. Don't forget to give it sufficient water, because it dries quickly from the warmth of the sun. It is easiest to grow in a plastic pot. Winter temperature should be at least 60° F. Propagate through cuttings kept under glass or plastic.

Bougainvillea ▶▶

Best known as a houseplant in the shrub form B. glabra sanderiana. It requires a good deal of care if you wish to keep it. Summer outside, in a sunny and warm spot; winter inside, at a temperature of 40-50° F. Keep it dry from the beginning of November. Many leaves will fall off. Spray the wood with water now and then to keep it healthy. In March, repot and place in a warm spot. The more sun it receives, the earlier it will bloom.

Bromeliads ▶

A large group of plants that includes strong and attractive kinds for houseplants. In a natural state, most bromeliads live on trees, with their roots in a very light mixture of rotting leaves and the like. Other types (Ananas, Cryptanthus) grow in the ground or between rocks. Every bromeliad rosette blooms only once, afterward forming a side shoot that, 1 to 3 years later, will bloom again. It is therefore easy to see why these side shoots should not be removed from the mother plant too early. If the plant fails to bloom after $2\frac{1}{2}$-3 years, it can be helped along by being placed in a plastic bag with a couple of healthy apples. The ethylene gas formed by the apples will encourage growth of the flowers. Leave the plant in the closed bag for two days. (It goes without saying that such an exceptional method helps only plants that have been through a healthy growing period. Unhealthy shoots can never be brought into bloom.) Most varieties need very humid, warm surroundings; but a few, such as Bilbergia nutans, are known for their indestructibility. Use rain water if possible, because lime is very damaging.

Cacti ▶

There are thousands of different varieties of cacti in all forms. Most have spines and are rather squat of form; but some have wide, leaflike stalks, or even true leaves. Many cacti form very beautiful flowers easily. The culture of almost all kinds will succeed only if they summer in full, warm sunlight and get sufficient water, preferably rain water. In the winter they should be kept very cold (45-50° F.) and no water should be given. Even under these conditions, almost all kinds will grow well and bloom richly. A few exceptions are so strong that they can even withstand winters in warm places and still bloom. But these are not the most attractive examples.

Cacti don't grow in sand and stone, as many people think. Soil that is rather humus but still contains lime is the best. A prepackaged special soil for cacti is available occasionally. Small types should be repotted every spring; larger types can remain longer in the same soil. During the growing period, regular fertilizing is necessary, preferably with a special cactus fertilizer that contains little nitrogen. To avoid rapid drying out in the small pots, cultivation in plastic pots is recommended. Although some forms of cacti can be propagated through cuttings, propagation is usually best from seeds. Seed is available from specialized nurseries. For the development of the seeds, it is necessary to keep them in a room that has a temperature at floor level of 80-85° F. After a few months they can be planted out, and after that it will be about 1-3 years, sometimes longer, before the cacti flower.

See also Rhipsalidopsis *and* Zygocactus.

Caladium ▶

These attractive leafy plants will last only a short time if kept in a warm room. Air that is too dry can cause the plant to fail quickly. Spraying with water can keep it healthy much longer. In September stop giving water so that the foliage will die. During the winter, keep the root dry in the pot at a temperature of about 65° F. Repot in the spring and bring into growth again.
Propagate by separating the roots. Every piece must have at least one eye.

Calathea ▶▶

Plants that are often confused with Maranta. Some kinds, such as C. lancifolia, with smaller, longer leaves; C. makoyana, oval, flecked leaves; and C. ornata Sanderiana (*photo*), are very strong and do extremely well if they are sprayed now and then. For other types, the air in the home is generally too dry.

Calceolaria ▶

This is a typical spring plant that is grown in great quantities in Holland at that time of year. There are various kinds with flowers of yellow, orange, red, purple, or violet, usually speckled. The plants are grown from seed that is planted in the ground in the previous year from May to July.
Although it makes a delightful gift, Calceolaria is unlikely to last very long. Once the flowers are gone it is best to throw the plant away, for keeping it is practically impossible. You can keep the flowers a fairly long time by keeping the plant as cool as possible, and now and then giving it a liquid fertilizer. If it stands in a draft, it may become diseased.

Campanula (Bellflower) ▶▶

An easy houseplant which tends to hang over the side of the pot. Usually white flowers, although the variety C. isophylla mayii are blue. Prune after blossoming and place in a light, cool place. Give little water. Repot in the spring and start it growing again. Two- or three-year-old plants have the most attractive blossoms; therefore take regular cuttings so as to always have plants this young. Yellow leaves indicate too much dryness or too much sun. Fertilize and cut off the dead flower areas every two weeks during the growing season.

Ceropegia (Rosary Plant) ▶

An unusually strong hanging plant that, unlike most other succulents, grows well with little light in locations such as in front of a north window. The vines can easily become 6 feet long. The tiny, lanternlike flowers generally appear at the end of the summer. The Ceropagia forms tubers in the soil and along the stems of older plants, which makes propagation very simple: just remove a tuber and pot it in another pot, half in and half out of the soil.

Don't give too much water. This plant can survive a few weeks of total dryness, but too much moisture kills it.

Chlorophytum (Spider Plant) ▶▶

Also a hanging plant that begins by growing straight up. When the flowers bloom, the long stems begin to hang down and from the ends of these, new plants form which, in turn, can also blossom. There are several varieties available which resemble each other. The usual green type can survive dim light; the type with white, striped leaves is prettier, but needs twice as much light. Propagate by removing the young plants.

Chrysanthemum ▶

Special growing techniques have produced chrysanthemums that can be kept small enough to grow in a pot. These can be kept for a few weeks or even a few months in front of a light window. Away from the window, the flowers last a shorter time. If the chrysanthemum seems to be doing poorly in the house, plant it in the garden, although there it will grow a great deal taller before blossoming again. In most cases, however, the plant is not winter hardy.

Cissus (Treebine and Grape Ivy) ▶▶

The ordinary C. antarctica, the larger one shown in the photo, is a climbing plant that can, with good care, cover an entire wall. The plant with the attractively flecked leaves is C. discolor, a delicate kind, which needs more light, more warmth, and a higher humidity. It is used in window boxes, but seldom survives long. This is in contrast to C. antarctica, which always lasts if the soil is not too acid. Put the plant in ordinary flower soil and add some lime. In August, propagate by keeping cuttings in a warm place.

See also Rhoicissus.

Citrus (Calamondin Orange) ▶

The best orange tree for use as a houseplant is a special dwarf species, known as C. microcarpa, or C. mitis. You can grow an orange tree by taking the pit of an ordinary orange and putting it into the ground, but such a plant will take years to produce fruit. The plant should summer in a place with lots of light and warmth, outside, if possible. When flowers appear on the plant, distribute the pollen with a brush to make sure it will produce fruit. It may take about a year before the fruit will be a good color. During the winter, the orange tree should be placed in a cooler part of the house, where the temperature is 45-50° F.

Clivia (Kafir Lily) ▶▶

Starting at the beginning of October, give the Clivia less water until the stalk is about 6 inches long. Then, once again give the normal amount, always at room temperature and, if possible, using distilled or rain water. Repot, if necessary, right after the plant blossoms. Give a soluble plant food every two weeks from the beginning of April until the end of August. If you don't pick the flower, seeds will form, and this weakens the plant. The seeds often take as long as 10 months to ripen. Instead of using seeds, propagate this plant by removing the young plants from the base of the adult plant as they form.

Codiaeum (Croton) ▶

In most cases, this leafy plant will grace your home for only a short time. After a few months, the dryness of the air indoors will cause the plant to decline and eventually to die. Spraying doesn't solve the problem, but the plant does last longer in a window box. Next in importance to moist air for this plant are warmth and a great deal of light (but not sun). An easy plant to raise in a plant window or a greenhouse. There are wide-leaved and narrow-leaved forms in various hues. Reproduce with cuttings taken in the spring and set to root in a warm greenhouse.

Coleus ▶▶

This is an easy-to-grow, rewarding plant. There are many color variations, all the result of crosses of older versions of the plant. To keep the shape and colors of this plant attractive, don't let it get too old. Once the blue flowers have appeared, the Coleus quickly becomes unattractive. Take frequent cuttings, preferably three times a year. These will root easily.
During the winter, when there is less light, the plant grows slowly but is still alive.

Columnea ▶

Although the Columnea thrives best in a humid area, some kinds can grow reasonably well in a heated room. The pictured C. x banksii is the most important of these. The plants grow best in a very light soil, such as that used for orchids. For rich blooms, a rest period in a cool place (55-60° F.) is necessary during December and January. The balance of the year a temperature between 65-70° F. is suitable and the plant should be sprayed often. Do not water with tap water. Columnea can only be propagated in a heated, closed greenhouse at 70-75° F. Cut the stalks in pieces about 2 inches long and put them in a mixture of 50 percent sand and 50 percent peat moss. The ideal growing medium for these plants consists of sphagnum, some leaf meal, and pieces of charcoal.

Cordyline (Dracaena) ▶▶

The difficulty with this plant is that the bottom leaves are almost always lost because of air that is too dry. Frequent spraying helps, and the Cordyline lives longer when planted with other plants. Bald plants can be air layered by making a cut in the stem. Damp moss wrapped in plastic can then be attached to the cut stem. Keep the mossball damp, but provide less water in the pot. After roots are formed, cut off the stem under the mossball and pot the new short plant.

Crassula ▶

This type of succulent is available in hundreds of varieties. Many of these are highly suitable for use as houseplants if you remember to keep the plant in full sunlight during the summer. Water should be given regularly, and now and then a feeding, preferably with cactus fertilizer because that contains less nitrogen. Blooming types require rest in the winter in a cold spot (45-50° F.) and almost complete dryness. Other types can be permitted to grow during the winter.

Crossandra (Firecracker-flower) ▶▶

A rich and long-blooming plant, which is difficult, however, to raise in the home because of its need for humid air. Frequent spraying can help, but the Crossandra only feels really at home in a small greenhouse or flower window. It is best to start new plants from cuttings every year in such a spot. Flowers cut from this plant last fairly long in water.

Cyclamen ▶

A plant which prefers a cool place where the air is not too dry, conditions that do not prevail in most living rooms. Placing the plant against the window, where it is generally cooler, can help keep the flowers and leaves from becoming limp, but better still is a more ventilated location. Water regularly, and once a week dunk in a fertilizer solution. If the plant is in a plastic pot, avoid giving too much water. After blossoms appear, give less water until all the leaves wither. After another 4 weeks of dryness, place the tuber in a somewhat larger pot and slowly bring it into growth again. Keep as cool as possible, without direct sunlight, and regularly spray the leaves.

The best-known Cyclamen has perfectly round flowers; but there are also types with fringed flower petals, horizontal standing petals, double-flower forms, and so forth. Small flowered variations which bloom richly and have highly scented blossoms are very new. Cyclamen lasts well as a cut flower.

Cyperus (Umbrella Plant) ▶▶

The plant is strong and easy to grow, and the $1\frac{1}{2}$-4 foot tall C. alternifolius, shown in the photo, is very decorative. This plant must stand with its base in a pan of water to which necessary fertilizer can be added. It is also advisable to spray the leaves now and then. The low (1 foot) C. diffusus must not stand in water and requires a somewhat higher temperature. Propagate with cuttings placed in water.

Dieffenbachia (Dumb-cane, Tuftroot) ▶

Most kinds prefer humid warmth and languish in dry room air, but some strong types last very well and grow to be quite large. In a window box, where the atmosphere is always more humid, this plant usually does nicely. Do not forget to feed. In the winter, you can keep the plant somewhat cooler, but not below 55° F. Propagate with cuttings of the stem in a warm spot.

Dipladenia ▶▶

A very sensitive plant that grows by climbing. Once again room air that is too dry is the usual cause of failure. Very frequent spraying helps somewhat. From November to February give less water at about 55° F., then keep it as warm as possible and feed it regularly until the beginning of August. This plant blossoms in the summer. In the autumn it can be severely pruned if desired.

Dizygotheca
(Threadleaf, False Aralia) ▶

Dizygotheca elegantissima, which is its official name, is a very strong and easy plant to grow; its only difficulty comes from air that is too dry. When this condition exists, the plant will lose its lowest leaves; but this is not necessarily always a handicap, as in a suitable pot even a bald stem doesn't look too unattractive. In a window box, lower plants can hide the baldness completely. You can avoid this loss of leaves for a longer time by spraying often.

Dracaena ▶▶

A very common foliage plant with leaves that are often rosettes, frequently showing an attractive design. Dracaena sanderiana, one example, has long stems covered with leaves that are green with white stripes. The thickset rosette of D. fragrans, with yellow stripes on the leaf, looks like a bromeliad. The leaves of D. deremensis (*photo*) are still more colorful, with very light stripes on the slender leaves. D. marginata has lovely dark-green, very slim leaves and later forms a long, thin stalk. D. godseffiana grows more as a bush and has oval leaves flecked with white.

Echeveria ▶

A succulent plant with thick, fleshy leaves that grow in spirals along the very short stem, creating a rosette. Various kinds are available in flower shops; the pictured E. setosa is perhaps the best known. In the summer this type likes to be outside, preferably in full sun. In winter it prefers a cool place to grow (not below 45° F., however) and little water. Blossoms come in the late spring. Propagate by seeds or by planting young rosettes.

Epiphyllum (Orchid Cacti) ▶▶

This plant is popular because of its very large flowers in splendid color. You can buy young plants at a special cactus nursery; they are relatively inexpensive. The culture is fairly easy to follow. In the summer keep the plant outside if possible, somewhat sheltered, and give fertilizer and water regularly until the first of August. In September bring it indoors, prune the longest shoot somewhat, and from mid-December to the beginning of February keep in a not-too-warm place and give little water. The leaves should be sprayed often. The plant flowers around May. Do not move the plant or the buds will fall off. Propagate with cuttings.

Euphorbia milii, or E. splendens (Crown of Thorns) ▶

An easy houseplant that requires a sunny window. Older plants can become very large and are exceptionally decorative. Euphorbia blossoms at various times, but generally during the spring. The flowers have a prickly stem.

At unexpected times, this plant can drop its leaves. This can happen if you neglect to water just once. But don't be upset by this, because it is part of the nature of Euphorbia to rest now and then. Give little or almost no water for around a month. When light green leaves again appear, slowly increase the water. This is also the best time to repot the plant. After that, it will probably bloom. Propagation is easy through cuttings from the top shoots that have first been allowed to dry out a little. Remember that the white sap is poisonous.

Euphorbia pulcherrima (Poinsettia) ▶▶

Occasionally called the Christmas Rose, although that is really the name of Helleborus niger, a plant that is almost never grown now for home culture. The poinsettia has become very popular recently, especially at Christmas but also at other seasons. The rose, red, or occasionally white, bracts — which are not actually petals — last a long time, especially those of the newest varieties. Give the plant water at room temperature, and now and then some houseplant fertilizer. Though maintaining the plant is difficult, you sometimes can do so by letting it rest a few months until it is dry and the leaves fall off, and then starting its growth again. After repotting, give it a great deal of sun, eventually place it outside, and fertilize well.

Fatshedera ▶

At the beginning of this century the Hedera was crossed with the Fatsia, creating this extremely strong plant. The climbing method of growth is inherited from the ivy, but it is possible to make the plant grow out more to the sides by pruning at the top now and then. Propagate with cuttings from the top.

Fatsia ▶▶

This is still called Aralia by many older nurseries. See also Dizygotheca, which is called False Aralia. The Fatsia is very sturdy, especially in fairly cool surroundings. It can withstand winter temperatures of 40° F., or even freezing point, provided the ground is dry. The more decorative form is more sensitive, needing ample li ʰt and warmth to survive. Propagate with seeds.

Ficus (India Rubber-plant) ▶

The very well-known F. elastica (rubber plant) is found in many homes. It is an easy grower, and forms few branches naturally unless you prune the top. Soil that is too damp is more damaging than soil that is too dry. Various fancier forms are available, but they need a great deal of light to stay attractive, while the ordinary rubber plant can survive in dim light.

In addition to the above-mentioned plant there are a number of other very strong varieties, of which the most important are: F. benjamina — $1\frac{1}{2}$-$3\frac{1}{2}$ inches long, with shiny green leaves — grows tall, is very decorative, and grows quickly everywhere; F. diversifolia has small, triangular leaves and bears round, yellow-green fruits; F. lyrata, an unusually decorative type, has deeply veined, lyre-shaped leaves which, with good care, can become 15 inches long; F. pumila (F. repens) is a climbing plant, with small, heart-shaped leaves; F. radicans is also a climbing plant, but it has larger leaves, 3-6 inches long and oval in form. Propagation is fairly easy with cuttings, but extra warmth is necessary.

Fittonia ▶

In newly planted boxes you may see this plant with its attractively veined leaves, but if you look again after a few months it will have shriveled. This is due to its great need for humid air, which is almost impossible to achieve in a heated room. The best location for it is in a greenhouse or terrarium. The type with silver graining is called F. verschaffeltii argyroneura; that with rose-red veins, F. verschaffeltii Pearcei.

Fuchsia ▶▶

The Fuchsia is an extremely rewarding plant that is very popular at present. Specialized nurseries keep a large variety on hand and you can obtain young plants for fairly low prices. For good growth the right soil mixture is very important. The various kinds that are used generally include some lime or clay. In summer, put the Fuchsia in a somewhat sheltered but still warm place. The windowsill is fine, but the garden is often too drafty for the more sensitive types. For them, a greenhouse may be best.

You can take cuttings throughout the summer. Roots form very easily if the cuttings are kept warm.

Gynura (Velvetplant) ▶

A common houseplant with velvetlike foliage in distinctive colors. This plant is easy to grow in a warm room, but do not let it become too old as young plants taken from cuttings are more attractive. Fortunately, it is very simple to make cuttings of the Gynura: cut off 4-inch pieces from the top, remove the lowest leaves from them, and place them in a growing medium of sand and peat moss. Golden-yellow flowers appear in the autumn on older plants.

Hedera (Ivy) ▶▶

The ordinary green Hedera helix (English Ivy), which also grows in the garden, is a strong plant that is easy to raise as a houseplant in cool locations. Too much warmth makes the plant less attractive. As a houseplant, the most common are the varieties with attractively colored foliage, such as Herald. Photographed is the very popular H. canariensis Variegata. Like all colorful plants, this type needs more light than the ordinary green Hedera helix. Cuttings from the top can best be taken in September, although they also succeed in other months.

Hibiscus ▶

This commonly grown houseplant can grow very large, having hundreds of blossoms in yellow or rose, single or double, every year. If you want such a large plant, your best choice is the single-flowered red because it is the strongest. Be sure the pot is large enough, and dunk the plant every week during the summer in water containing fertilizer.

It's a good idea to let the plant rest during the winter. Keep the temperature at 55-60° F., giving just enough water to avoid having it dry out completely. In the spring, prune the plant as necessary, then repot and start growth again.

Propagate in the spring in a warm place with cuttings from young shoots.

Hippeastrum (Amaryllis) ▶▶

In order to keep this bulb plant after it flowers, keep the plant in full light, so that the leaves will grow well. Give houseplant fertilizer every week. In June the plant can be placed in the garden, sheltered from the full sun. Continue giving fertilizer until the first of August. In September, give no more water. When the leaves are entirely dead, set the pot with the bulb in a cool, dark closet (50-55° F.). At the beginning of February, replace the topsoil, set in a rather warm spot, and give water again. The flower stalk should speedily appear. Once every two years carefully repot the plant before it blooms.

Hoya (Waxplant) ▶

There are two kinds of Hoya used as houseplants. H. bella, rarely used in America, has smaller, fleshy leaves, which grow in a hanging fashion, so that this is a plant to put in a special hanging pot in front of a somewhat sheltered window. H. carnosa (*photo*) is generally raised in a pot to which a circle of wire is attached, as is also done with Stephanotis (page 56). The long stems of this climber can then be trained onto the wire circle. The plant should not be moved because this will cause the buds to fall off. Give little fertilizer, and watch out for pests. The pot must have good drainage and the plant should be kept warm in winter.

Hydrangea ▶▶

The houseplant Hydrangea, which is often grown in gardens, too, is a typical spring gift plant. Do not put it in the sun, for this will make the leaves curl. To help the flowers last longer, keep the plant in a cool place, if possible. Give sufficient lime-free water. If you wish to keep the hydrangea, prune it back at the end of May and put it outside in a light, sheltered place. It's a good idea to cover the soil with plastic to keep it from drying out. Fertilize well until the end of August. Keep cool and fairly dry during the winter, then move to a warmer spot in February.

Hypocyrta ▶

H. glabra is the correct name of this humble plant with its dark-green, leatherlike leaves. The plump orange flowers bloom throughout the year except during the autumn, appearing in the axils of the leaves. The plant as a whole resembles the Columnea. A great deal of light is necessary for bud formation, and full sun is good for the plant.
Two-inch sections of the stalk can be rooted easily.

Impatiens ▶▶

Because this plant is so easy to grow during the summer and can easily be propagated by cuttings, it is rarely necessary to buy it in a flower shop. The only thing it needs to succeed is plenty of light, full sunlight when necessary, and sufficient water and food. A great deal of warmth is not needed and the plants do well outdoors. The usual variety has green leaves, and white to dark-red flowers.
The species I. petersiana is bronze-colored and always has red flowers.

Iresine (Bloodleaf) ▶

This plant is common in window boxes but is also used alone on the windowsill. It is liked for its contrasting, blood-red leaves. In the summer it can live outside, in full sunlight.

Many varieties are cultivated, but the one in the photograph is probably the best known.

From time to time, Iresine must be started again from cuttings, because older plants grow unattractive. The cuttings will form roots even in water. Put several cuttings in one pot and cut the tops back a few times to obtain stocky plants.

Kalanchoe ▶▶

Some nurseries withhold light in order to force the Kalanchoe into early bloom, a method which enables some varieties to bloom in the autumn. A plant treated this way is somewhat "befuddled," however, and keeping it is difficult. If you do succeed in keeping it, the plant will bloom a few months later the following year. After it blooms you can give the Kalanchoe several weeks rest; then repot if necessary and place it in front of a light window for the summer, providing sufficient fertilizer.

Maranta (Arrowroot) ▶

The variety M. leuconeura kerchoviana, or M. bicolor (the lower plant in the photo), has about 10 dark flecks on its bottle-green leaves. The variety M. leuconeura massangeana, which you see at the top of the photo, has even more attractively marked leaves, but is more difficult to grow in the home. Both are happier in a well-filled window box because the atmosphere there is somewhat more humid. If their location is rather dark, place a lamp above them during the winter, preferably throughout the night. This may help them to grow a little better.

Monstera (Ceriman) ▶▶

One of the strongest houseplants. If the Monstera once becomes accustomed to a certain location, it will manage with less light and will also be able to withstand dry air. Warmth is very necessary, but that is rarely lacking in the ordinary living room. The more the plant has things to its liking, the larger and more attractive the leaves. With good care many air roots will form, which you can either cut off or lead to the soil in the pot for better absorption of food. Don't forget to repot this reliable plant now and then, and also give it fertilizer during the summer.

Nephrolepis (Sword Ferns) ▶

The secret of growing one of these plants successfully in the house lies in sufficient feeding. The plant must also be repotted when necessary. If, despite this good care, the plant fails to produce new leaves and the old ones die back, give it a rest period. Give less water, but avoid letting it dry out completely, and cut all the old leaves off. After 5 or 6 weeks the plant should once again begin to grow, at which point start once again to give water and fertilizer. Propagate through runners.

Nerium (Oleander) ▶▶

The correct Latin name is Nerium oleander. It is a plant with matte-green, lancet-shaped leaves and lovely flowers that can often be seen growing outdoors in Southern Europe, Florida, and California, where it blossoms throughout the summer. To raise it as a houseplant, it is best to have it spend the winter in a cool place (40-45° F.) where the pot will be neither too wet nor too cold. If the plant spends the winter in a too-warm location, it will not flower well. At the beginning of June, place the Oleander in a sheltered corner in full sunlight. Take care to give sufficient water and plant fertilizer during the period of growth. Bring the plant indoors at the end of September.
Propagate with cuttings, which will root in water.

Palms ▶

All types of palms are grown as houseplants, but here we are concerned only with those requiring similar care. The larger ones are unusually decorative, but are suitable only for huge houses. In the summer, palms can be placed outdoors in a sheltered place, preferably not in full sunlight.
Palms grow best in a deep pot or tub with good drainage and a clay or lime soil, so be sure to provide a lime-containing light soil. With regular fertilizing you can ensure the formation of many new leaves; then the old leaves can be removed. Large palms can often last a long time with a fairly low temperature or insufficient light. But after a while they must once again be given proper care in a greenhouse or be placed by a window; otherwise, various difficulties will arise. Larger plants do not have to be repotted every year. The most suitable palms for the home are Chamaedorea, Howea (Kentia), Syagrus, and Phoenix.

Pandanus (Screw-pine) ▶

The most common is P. veitchii, a plant that in the course of time can become very large and exceptionally decorative. The leaves spiral out from a short stem and the leaf edges are finely marked. You must keep this plant comfortably warm and spray it very often. A little sunlight does no harm to the Pandanus, but the strong sun of noon must be avoided.

Paphiopedilum (Orchid) ▶▶

The Paphiopedilum shown here is representative of the large orchid family, which we shall treat as a whole. The best for culture as a houseplant are varieties of Bletilla, Coelogyne, Cymbidium (small types), Lycaste, Odontoglossum, Oncidium, and Paphiopedilum. There are, of course, home-gardening experts who have raised other orchids in the home, but their successes are exceptional. The most suitable spot for orchid culture is a window facing west, which will have sun only during the evening. Average room temperature is fine, but you must raise the humidity as much as possible through frequent spraying. The plants should be placed in very special soil that your nursery will mix for you, and in a well-drained pot. You should water, and water often, with rain water, except during the rest periods. These rules hold true for all kinds of orchids.

Passiflora (Passion-flower) ▶

The Passion-flower develops very long stems, which, as a rule, are bound around a metal hoop to keep it at least manageable in a room. Be careful to grow this plant in a cool, well-ventilated place – in the winter at 40° F., and in the summer preferably in a sunny spot in front of an open window. In certain European countries people raise this plant successfully against a south wall where the temperature may go as low as 5° F. If you try this, be certain to cover the roots with a mulch such as straw or leaves. Propagate with cuttings of the young shoots in a warm place.

Pelargonium (Geranium) ▶▶

The best culture for all Geraniums is to place cuttings in a sandy soil in August. As the cuttings form roots, set them in a somewhat larger pot and in October place in a cool spot (40-45° F.) to spend the winter. Throw away the old plant. In March, repot the plants if they need it. At the end of May the plants can be repotted, if necessary, for the third time, and moved to the garden or a balcony, where they will come into bloom quickly. With regular fertilizing, these flowers can be kept until autumn. If you follow these instructions, you will never have to buy new plants, and you can even give cuttings away.

Pellaea (Cliff-brake) ▶

Although it is not generally known, these plants, with their glistening green, round leaves, belong to the fern family. You can tell this by the brown spore bunches that appear on the bottom of the leaves of older plants. This plant never flowers. The pictured P. rotundifolia is the most common; but there is another type, P. viridis, that looks much more like a fern with its long-reaching, strongly incised leaves.

Peperomia ▶▶

There are many different kinds of Peperomia, of which at least twenty are quite common. Though not spectacular plants, they are very suitable for window boxes. They do not need a great deal of water and some are even succulents, which means that they store water in their leaves.

Be sure that the temperature does not fall under 60° F., and try to provide as much humid air as possible because these plants, which come from the tropics, thrive best in such conditions.

Propagate with cuttings or by division.

Philodendron ▶

Attractive houseplants, some of which can become very large. The best known is P. cordatum, or P. scandens (*photo*), a climbing kind with rather small (5 inches maximum), heart-shaped leaves; it is very strong and grows easily anywhere.

More decorative are such kinds as P. erubescens, which has thicker stems and long, arrow-shaped leaves up to 10 inches, that appear red. The bract is purple. P. melanochrysum has large, narrow, velvet-green leaves with white veins.

P. panduriforme has large leaves with two round lobes at the base; it also grows very large. P. sagittifolium Ilsemanii has leaves of white flecked with rose. All types should be sprayed as often as possible, fertilized well, and not kept in too much darkness. Repot if possible every spring.

Phlebodium, or Polypodium (Polypody Ferns) ▶▶

Relatives of the well-known staghorn fern, Platycerium. Although less common, it grows quite well in the home. P. aureum mandaianum, with irregular wavy foliage, is especially attractive. Typical is the creeping, light-brown, scaled root mass, which goes through the entire pot.

It may take time for these ferns to feel at home, but leave the plant alone and keep the soil damp, not letting it become too dry or too wet. After a while it will begin to grow by itself. Propagate by division.

Pilea (Aluminum Plant) ▶

Most commonly seen as a foliage plant in window boxes is P. cadierei (*photo*), which can be kept for some time in a room but will never be a really beautiful, healthy plant unless it is placed in a greenhouse or window garden. The completely reddish-green P. involucrata, or P. spruceana, with its bumpy leaves, is somewhat easier to care for, especially as far as light is concerned.

Pittosporum ▶▶

A less well-known houseplant that nevertheless offers possibilities as a foliage plant for a slightly heated room. Good light is necessary; the temperature must not be too high, and in winter may even be as low as 40-45° F. In the summer the plant can be placed in a sheltered spot outside.

With a little luck the Pittosporum will bloom very attractively, with white or cream scented flowers.

Of the various types, P. tobira, P. eugenioides (*photo*), and P. undulatum are the most suitable for use as houseplants.

Propagation is generally with seeds, but can also be accomplished with cuttings of young shoots at the end of the summer.

Platycerium (Staghorn Ferns) ▶

It's amazing how well these ferns do in dry, heated rooms, perhaps because of the protective wax coating that covers the leaf. Don't polish the wax off in a fit of house-cleaning!

The plant grows very well on a piece of tree bark into which a ball of damp moss or orchid soil is placed, but this makes watering somewhat difficult. The best thing to do is to remove the entire plant and dampen the moss in water. Don't forget to dissolve some fertilizer in the water when you do this.

Primula (Primrose) ▶▶

These plants are not long-lived, although P. obconica, the type that causes some people to break out in a rash, can last fairly long if you put it in the garden in the summer and keep it damp and sheltered. P. praenitens (P. sinensis, Chinese Primrose) can be grown from seeds in a greenhouse. P. malacoides (Fairy Primrose) blooms in the winter with long stems on which the flowers appear in rows. In the early spring we find P. vulgaris (P. acaulis, English Primrose), a low plant with flowers in vivid, almost artistic, tints. This type can also be placed in the garden as it is fairly hardy.

All Primulas like a great deal of water; indeed, P. vulgaris is noted for its thirst. So it is best to grow these plants in plastic pots that are watered a bit less often. Propagation is generally from seeds. Photo shows P. obconica at top, P. vulgaris at bottom left, and P. malacoides at bottom right.

Pteris ▶

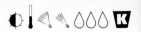

The best-known and most typical kind is P. cretica, or Stove Fern, which has light-striped, incised leaves in countless variations. It is a very suitable plant for window boxes, and can also be grown well in pots. Be sure to provide enough moisture and give it fertilizer throughout the summer.
P. tremula, or Trembling Brake, is more of an "ordinary" fern with overhanging, strongly incised leaves. There are many more kinds in the shops.
Propagate by division.

Rechsteineria (Corytholoma) ▶▶

This plant requires a culture similar to the Sinningia (page 56) and has tuberous roots that should winter at a temperature of at least 50° F. in the pot, completely dry. Before that time, around September, gradually stop giving water so that all the leaves fall off.

Rhaphidophora, or Scindapsus (Ivy-arum) ▶

Though Rhaphidophora is the new name, Scindapsus is the one most frequently used. This climber (or hanging plant) is certainly the strongest of the fancier plants. In dark places the leaves become somewhat less attractive, but the plant hangs on to the bitter end. Because the thick leaves can absorb some moisture, it is not a disaster if you forget to give it water for a week. Sufficient warmth is necessary, however. Propagate from cuttings.

Rhipsalidopsis (Easter Cactus) ▶▶

The plant looks very much like the Schlumbergera bridgesii, or Christmas Cactus, also a member of the cactus family. Blossom time, as the name suggests, is usually around Easter.
After blooming, when the plant is less interesting, it is best placed in a sheltered spot in the garden when there is no danger of frost. If necessary, repot. Be sure to give sufficient water, and fertilize now and then. At the end of September bring it inside to a not-too-warm place. In December and January place it in a cool (40-45° F.) and rather dry spot for formation of buds. In March (or earlier), when the buds can be seen, place it in a warmer spot and give more water. Propagate with pieces of the leaves.

Rhoeo ►

At first sight, this plant may remind you of the Bromeliads, but it does not belong to this family. Nevertheless, the growing conditions are rather similar: humid warmth is best. The Rhoeo can endure conditions in the home rather well, especially if placed in a planter with other plants. The flowers are more unusual than attractive; they appear in shell-formed bracts, pressed against the base.

Rhoicissus (Evergreen Treebine) ►►

This is a relative of Cissus (page 22), also called Cissus rhombifolia. The plant is strong and survives in the middle of the room, even if it is 12 feet from a window. The difference between it and the Cissus is the three small leaves beneath the simple leaves.

This vinelike plant likes an open, lime-rich soil. Therefore replant it in a pot with the soil mixture given on page 8.

Propagation is very simple. Shoots of 4 inches in length form roots easily if you place them in a small pot, cover with a plastic bag, and keep warm.

Rochea ►

Superficially, this plant looks like an enlarged model of the Kalanchoe (page 40), but the leaf is very different: narrow, small, and placed on the stems in thick rows. The Rochea is also a succulent and blooms in the summer, so it's important to keep it cool in the winter (40-45° F.) in a well-lighted spot, while giving little water. In the spring, when the plant again begins to grow, be careful not to give too much moisture. After it blossoms, prune off the flower shoots. Propagate in August from cuttings of the shoots.

Saintpaulia (African Violet) ►►

Attractive, richly blooming plants for the home or for a warmed greenhouse. They require a great deal of humidity in the air, which can most easily be supplied by placing several Saintpaulia together in a plastic terrarium. Regular fertilizing is necessary during the period of bloom.

After blooming, the plants have earned their rest, so give them one at a temperature of 55-60° F. with less water.

Propagating is successful from pieces of the leaves. Place the leaves straight up in a mixture of sand and some peat moss, with a little of the stem exposed. Under glass or plastic, at a minimum temperature of 65° F., roots develop very rapidly. Sometimes roots develop even in a glass of water.

Sansevieria ►

There is no question but that this is the most indestructible of all houseplants. Even many weeks without water or a stay in the darkest corner of the room fails to kill it. Often, people give the Sansevieria too good a location — in front of the window in the sun — which causes the leaves to become light yellow and less attractive. The most beautiful kind is the yellow-striped S. trifasciata laurentii that you see at the left of the photo. Less well known is the low form, S. trifasciata hahnii (*photo*, *right*). There is also a yellow decorated form, the Golden Hahnii.
Propagation of Sansevieria is best done by division.

Saxifraga (Mother of Thousands) ►►

There are many different kinds of Saxifraga that look quite different, but this S. sarmentosa Tricolor is the best known as a houseplant. The plant is very good for a rather light window where it has room to grow. Damp air is necessary, so if you spray the leaves now and then, it will be grateful. There is also another form of this Saxifraga that likes less light and warmth. The leaf is olive green with clear, silver-white veins.
Propagate by the cutting of runners.

Schefflera (Octopus Tree) ►

A strong foliage plant that is not very well known but with which you can have great success, especially in a window box, although it succeeds in a pot. The leaf is compound and consists of 7-8 individual leaflets.
The ideal temperature for this plant is between 55-60° F., so a cold hallway is usually more suitable than the living room, where the thermostat is often set too high.

Senecio (Cineraria) ►►

Though this plant is usually called Cineraria, its correct name is Senecio cruentus. The plant, in bloom, is seen in florist shops in the early spring and winter. If you want to enjoy the Cineraria, keep it cold. It is actually a garden plant for frost-free areas, and in room air the leaves quickly fall off. It is not worth keeping this plant unless you have a frost-free cold frame.
It's really best to grow new plants yourself from seed.

Sinningia (Gloxinia) ▶

Mostly known by the popular name of Gloxinia. A tuberous plant, usually sold in bloom in the spring. The plants have a terrific appetite; if you wish to enjoy them, you must always give them water to which fertilizer has been added and, moreover, you should dunk them once a week in water in which fertilizer is dissolved. After they blossom, slowly give less water until all the leaves are dried up. After that, the tuber can be left in the pot at a temperature of at least 40° F. Remove the old soil at the end of February and place the tuber, with some moist peat moss, in a plastic bag, and put in a warm spot. When you can tell from the shoots which is the top of the plant, pot it again in fertile soil. Extra light encourages early growth.

Solanum pseudo-capsicum (Jerusalem-cherry) ▶▶

Not to be confused with the orange tree, the Citrus (page 24). This bush has hard, shiny, orange-to-red, marblelike fruits. Some types have round, others oval, fruits. You will probably purchase this plant in the autumn or winter. Put the plant in as light and cool a place as possible. When the fruits fall off, probably in February, repot the plant and prune it a little. When growth begins again, prune the top once or twice so that the tree won't grow too weedy. If possible, put it outside at the end of May, in a warm spot with full sun. In the autumn, new fruits will develop.

Sparmannia (African Hemp) ▶

Now that the demand for large houseplants is on the increase, the Sparmannia is once again becoming popular. It is an excellent houseplant for warm and cool locations, and it becomes very large. Take care to use a suitable pot, or, rather, a tub. To blossom well, the plant should have rest in May, with little water given, and should eventually be placed in the garden. After 4-6 weeks cut the longest stem back as much as you wish, repot the plant, and bring it inside again or place it in a sunny spot. Propagate through cuttings in the spring.

Stephanotis ▶▶

Although this is really a plant for a greenhouse, many people have had great success with it as a houseplant. With good care, blooms appear every year, usually from about June to September. It's very important to keep this plant at a temperature no warmer than 50-55° F. during the winter and to water it very moderately. If you fail to do these things, the chance is great that the plant will become diseased. A lightly heated guest room is very suitable for a winter stay. In summer, when growth is strong, the Stephanotis can have a warmer location, but it will then also require good ventilation. Fertilize only sparingly. Propagate by cuttings in warm soil.

Streptocarpus (Cape Primrose)

A plant with extremely long leaves that will hang out of a pot. Therefore, instead of a pot use a large bowl, so that the leaves will extend over the soil and not dry out so quickly. In winter it's best to keep this plant in a cool place (55° F.) and give it very moderate amounts of water. Repot in the spring, move to a warmer spot, give it more water and, later, also fertilizer. The modern hybrids produce many blossoms in blue, purple-blue, lilac, rose, or white. As a rule, they are strongly veined.

You can easily propagate the Streptocarpus from cuttings. Cut the leaf through at the main stalk and place it flat on a mixture of peat moss and sand. Press the rib side into the soil and cover it. Under glass or plastic, at a temperature of 65-70° F., it will eventually form numerous new plants that can later be separated and planted in pots.

Syngonium ►►

A plant that strongly resembles the Philodendron (page 46) and requires similar care. A recognition point (in young plants) is the arrow-shaped leaves which have two "ears" at the base.

During the time of growth, air roots can form on the stems. If you lead these to a fertile medium, such as damp peat moss that is placed on a piece of bark, the leaves will become noticeably larger.

Tradescantia and Zebrina (Wandering Jew) ►

These plants resemble each other very much and belong to the same family, which is why we treat them together. Both have a method of growth that goes from creeping to hanging, and the leaves — often somewhat fleshy — almost enclose the stems. The top of the leaves may be striped in green and white, while the underside is often violet-colored.

These plants will grow very easily in almost any room. They are often used in window boxes. Too much water is harmful, and it is good to keep the plants somewhat cooler and drier in the winter. If the plant loses its attractiveness, grow new young plants in the spring from cuttings. Shoots of 4-5 inches will root easily.

Zygocactus (Thanksgiving Cactus) ►►

This member of the cactus family has violet-colored flowers that appear at Christmastime. When the plant has finished blooming, keep it inside for a time so that it can rest in a moderately warm room. You will quickly see new shoots develop on the stems. Do not overwater. At the end of May the Zygocactus can be placed in the garden in a sheltered spot. Give sufficient water and also houseplant fertilizer until the first of August. After that, do not give fertilizer but continue with water. In October, before the first frost, bring the plant in and place in a not-too-warm spot.

INDEX